# Bill Oddie's
## INTRODUCTION TO
# BIRDWATCHING

First published in 2002 by New Holland Publishers (UK) Ltd
London • Cape Town • Sydney • Auckland

2 4 6 8 10 9 7 5 3 1

Garfield House, 86-88 Edgware Road, London W2 2EA, United Kingdom
www.newhollandpublishers.com

80 McKenzie Street, Cape Town 8001, South Africa

Level 1/Unit 4, 14 Aquatic Drive, Frenchs Forest, NSW 2086, Australia

218 Lake Road, Northcote, Auckland, New Zealand

ISBN 1 85974  894 5 hardback
ISBN 1 84330 016 8 paperback

Publishing Manager: Jo Hemmings
Project Editor: Lorna Sharrock
Copy Editor: Sylvia Sullivan
Designer: Rosamund Saunders
Index: Janet Dudley
Production: Joan Woodroffe

Reproduction by Modern Age Repro House Ltd, Hong Kong
Printed and bound in Singapore by Tien Wah Press (Pte) Ltd

THE wildlife TRUSTS

# Bill Oddie's
## INTRODUCTION TO
# BIRDWATCHING

NH
NEW HOLLAND

# THE WILDLIFE TRUSTS

The Wildlife Trusts partnership is the UK's leading voluntary organization working, since 1912, in all areas of nature conservation. We have more than 343,000 members, and supporters include famous household names such as our vice president Bill Oddie.

The Wildlife Trusts protect wildlife for the future by managing in excess of 2,300 nature reserves, ranging from woodlands and peat bogs, to coastal habitats and wildflower meadows. We campaign tirelessly on behalf of all wildlife, including of course the multitude of bird species.

We run thousands of events, including dawn chorus walks and birdwatching activities, with projects for adults and children across the UK. Leicestershire and Rutland Wildlife Trust, with the RSPB, organises the British Birdwatching Fair at Rutland Water — now also home to Osprey. The Wildlife Trusts work to influence industry and government and also advise landowners.

As numbers of formerly common species plummet, we are urging people from all walks of life to take action, whether supporting conservation organisations in their work for birds, or taking a few small steps in their own lives.

By reading *Bill Oddie's Introduction to Birdwatching* you can discover some of the thrills of the natural world. Bill Oddie knows how to gently introduce the reader to the simple joys of watching and listening for the Songthrush, Skylark or Blackcap. For the more adventurous and patient there are stunning experiences ranging from the rare boom of Bitterns to the haunting cry of Manx Shearwater.

Whilst many birders choose to explore every corner of the British Isles, and beyond, for many novices the local park or back garden can provide a good starting point and be just as enjoyable.

A recent survey conducted by The Wildlife Trusts, in association with the *Daily Telegraph* and BBC's *Tomorrow's World*, asked people to tick off the wildlife they had seen in their garden over the previous year. The list included the Robin, Blackbird, Wren and House Sparrow. More than 66,000 people responded, confirming what experts had warned, for example that the House Sparrow had declined dramatically, and that for many species gardens had become the final refuge. Results also told us just how much people love watching wildlife, especially birds.

*The Wildlife Trusts partnership is a registered charity (number 207238). For membership, events, news and other details, please phone The Wildlife Trusts on 01636 677711, or log on to www.wildlifetrusts.org*

# CONTENTS

# INTRODUCTION

Ⅰt is customary for books like this one to start with a rave about how wonderful – beautiful, fascinating, entertaining, important – birds are. I'm not going to do that. I'm going to assume you think that anyway. I'm also going to assume that you are thinking of becoming a "real" birdwatcher. Well, my initial response to that is simply: "Yes. Go on, do it!"

I'm not going to analyze the appeal of birdwatching, but all I will say is that it has kept me intrigued, busy, happy and arguably sane for fifty years. It is quite simply a hobby for a lifetime. And I'm not the only one who thinks that. There are literally millions of birdwatchers all over the world and the number is growing daily.

I quote the editorial I was reading in the "business" magazine on a transatlantic flight recently (yes, that's how bored I got!) which stated: "Birding is the biggest growth leisure pursuit in the western world." That's marketing speak for "it's getting more and more popular!" So you'll be in good company.

Or will you? What exactly is a real birdwatcher? As opposed to someone who just enjoys watching birds. A recent audience analysis of my BBC series "Birding With Bill Oddie" concluded that about 90 per cent of my viewers "would not consider themselves real birdwatchers". Is that modesty, or embarrassment? I sometimes wonder if it is the latter. Let's face it, there are certain cliché images and stereotypes of the "typical birdwatcher", and maybe you don't fancy being labelled

accordingly. I've heard them, us – including me – labelled as "anoraks". I presume this implies that birdwatchers are rather boring,

Right: *Time was when you could identify a 'real birdwatcher' by his or her ownership of a telescope and a tripod. Not any more! They've all got them now.*

narrow-minded, and ramble on tediously about birds and nothing much else. Well, of course there *are* bird bores, but then there are bores in just about every area. As for literally wearing an anorak … very sensible, I'd say! If you are outdoors in all kinds of weather, it's just as well to wear some protective clothing. Added to which, I thought anoraks and woolly hats were rather hip these days – street cred gear, in fact.

But there really is no such thing as the typical birdwatcher. I honestly believe there can be very few other leisure pursuits that attract such a wide spectrum of types of people as birdwatching. I have met all kinds: millionaire businessmen, clergy, punks, hippies, young, old, all races and religions, and both sexes, and variations in between, all unified by their passion for birds. Indeed, I would go as far as to say that birdwatching

Left: *In fact, these people are breaking one of the basic birding rules: don't suddenly appear over the horizon. No doubt they were in pursuit of something really rare, and got over-excited. Now they've probably scared it away.*

is fantastic for bringing people together. Believe me, birders are all very different under their anoraks!

The other cliché image of modern birdwatching is of "twitchers". In fact, the media have hijacked this word and often use it to refer to any level of birdwatching. I recently appeared in a photo in a national newspaper along with Julian Pettifer and a bunch of youngsters who had designed a bird garden. We were all labelled as "twitchers", simply because the project had something to do with birds. Wrong! Twitching is in fact a specialized, specific and indeed rather extreme kind of birdwatching. It is first and foremost the pursuit of rarities.

## The true meaning of twitching

It is also invariably "mass" birding, when large crowds travel from far and wide and gather to tick off one – often small, dull,

but rare – bird. Not surprisingly, this sort of thing appeals to the media no end. The image of ranks and ranks of almost identical-looking bearded blokes with thousands of pounds worth of optical gear does undeniably make for an eye-catching photo in the paper, or "jokey" item at the end of the news. And if the behaviour of the twitchers gets a bit frantic, so much the better. Maybe the bird flies over the hill and the hordes race off in pursuit, or it flies off altogether and the late arrivals miss it and are reduced – sometimes literally – to tears. It happens. The emotions involved in twitching can be pretty extreme. In fact, that's where the word comes from. It was coined many many years ago among a then small group of rarity chasers, some of whom would get so over excited at the prospect of seeing a new bird, or so frantically nervous that they might miss it, that they would literally shake, palpitate or "twitch" with the emotion of the whole thing. It is certainly true that twitching can be stressful. It can also be expensive and time consuming. It is also pretty much male dominated. I can entirely appreciate that this all adds up to an image that puts off quite a number of people who may be considering becoming birdwatchers. Well, let me reassure you on several points. First and foremost, twitching is not "normal birdwatching", even if the media may mislead you into thinking it is. Secondly, as it happens, twitching can also be great fun. But thirdly – and most importantly – you don't have to go twitching at all to be a birdwatcher. In fact, if you are relatively new to birds, I'd go so far as to say that you shouldn't really go twitching … yet. (See chapter 9).

## It's whatever you want it to be

I hope I have convinced you that you don't have to conform to some cliché image. The truly splendid thing about birdwatching is that you really can enjoy it on whatever level you want. So, in a sense perhaps, there is no such thing as a "real" birdwatcher. There are, of course, let's call them, differing levels of ability. There are scientific ornithologists, field craft experts, people who know quite a bit, and people who know very little. However, I really do not believe that there is anybody that knows nothing at all about birds.

*Below: Feeding the ducks: many people's first contact with birds. They may behave as if they are tame (the ducks I mean), but the chances are that many of them are wild birds, looking for an easy meal.*

Here's another reason to be encouraged: you may feel that you are a complete beginner, but I bet you know more than you realize.

I am convinced that everyone has some small basic knowledge of and probably interest in birds. At the very least, we all notice them – they are surely the most conspicuous form of wildlife, be they pigeons in the park, Robins in the garden, or "sea gulls" on the beach. We are also introduced to them at a very early age. There can't be many of us who as toddlers – or even as babies in prams – weren't taken to feed the ducks. I and my three-year-old grandson recently visited the duck pond on Hampstead Heath near where I live in London. I call it a "duck pond", but of course the wildfowl that came for our crusts weren't just ducks. There were Canada Geese and Mute Swans, and Coots and Moorhens. What's more, within minutes my grandson realized this (and not just because I told him.) "That's a swan, isn't it, Grandad?" "Yes." "And that's a Canada Goose." That one surprised me, until I remembered that one of his babysitters was Canadian! "And what's that?" he asked, pointing at a Coot. He didn't know its name, but he knew it was something different. Now, I'm not saying he will become a birdwatcher, but he *was* already watching birds, and he was already beginning to identify them. We counted the different species we could see on the pond,

Below: *"They all look the same."* I think not! Ironically, the one that you may know best – the House Sparrow – is becoming worryingly scarce. The other two are Great Tit and Chaffinch.

are wonderful. Buy one now if you can afford it, or are curious, or confident that you are going to need it eventually, but – take my advice – in the early days, stick to the common birds.

A few field guides are illustrated with photographs rather than paintings. Logically, one might assume that photos would be more realistic and therefore more helpful, but I don't believe this is the case (and I think most birders agree with me). I suppose it is because a good artist can show you exactly what you need to know: each species in all plumages, posed to show off all its features, in perfect light, with no distracting background. Photographs may be more natural, but the very naturalism –

a distorted pose, shadows, or the orange effect of sunlight – can actually make the species less easily recognized. Added to which, even the most prolific photographic library probably hasn't got a slide of every British bird in every plumage. Having said that, there are some photographic guides that are extremely thorough and very pleasing. By all means buy one, for aesthetic reasons if nothing else, and as an extension to your illustrated guides, but if you asked me to choose between artwork and photos, I'd have to say artwork.

OK, so you've decided which guide you want to buy, or maybe you have already got it. You flick through it. A couple of things that may boggle you a bit: most guides begin

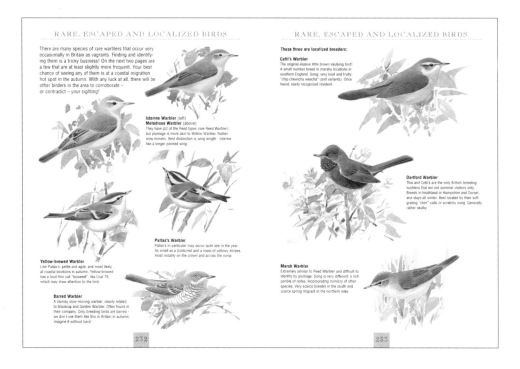

Below left and opposite above: *Willow Warbler.*
*Ironically, an illustration will often show a more*
*quintessentially accurate image than does a*
*photograph (no disrespect to photographers). Also*
*– be honest – there is something aesthetically*
*pleasing about beautiful bird paintings.*

Below and opposite below: *Common Chiffchaff.*
*There are some stunning photos too. Fortunately,*
*these two warblers - which, let's face it, look*
*almost identical - have completely different songs.*
*So that's the easiest way to tell them apart.*
*Even pretty-experienced birders sometimes refer*
*to them as 'willow/chiffs', unless the birds*
*are singing.*

# INSECT EATERS

# SEED EATERS

21

# ESSENTIAL GEAR

s well as a field guide, you will need a decent pair of binoculars ("bins" for short). Happily, this is another area where things really have got very good indeed. Mind you, there is such a huge range of types, styles, sizes and prices that you may feel rather confused over what to choose. The rule – again (I said I'd be repeating this) – is to buy from a specialist dealer. Don't buy from the local chemist, or even photographic shop. They may well have some good bins but they won't have a huge range, and the price is likely to be higher than at the specialist. These companies are run for and often by birdwatchers. You will find them advertised in the bird magazines (see page 137) or yellow pages. You will be able to get advice, go to the shop and try out different models, and possibly even be able to get a pair on approval so you can field test them.

Frankly, there is an awful lot of potential waffle about the various types of optical systems, specifications, dimensions and so on, and it's easy to feel a bit blinded by science. But remember that rule: don't bother with things you don't need to know. To help, I will simply run through the meaning of some of the figures you do need to know about!

**Magnification**. This is simple enough. All binoculars are clearly marked 7, 8, 10, or whatever the magnification is. This means what it implies: that the subject is magnified seven times or eight times or ten times. The ideal magnification for birdwatching is between 7 and 10 (inclusive). There will

Right: *Great Spotted Woodpecker using different magnification. From left to right: 6 x magnification, 9 x magnification and 12 x magnification (all at 6m range); close-up yes, but you'd have trouble holding the binoculars steady.*

also be a second number, for example, the bins may be marked 7 x 42 or 8 x 40. This second figure is (I think!) millimetres and refers somehow to lens sizes. You see, I don't really understand it and you don't need to either! (The man in the shop will explain if you want him to but you may remain slightly baffled, as I am.) What you do need to appreciate is that this second figure is to do with how wide and how bright the image is. There is a trade-off here. Generally speaking, the more you magnify, the less wide the picture will be, and it will also be less bright. It is honestly true that a smaller brighter image is often clearer and preferable to a big murky close up. A generally accepted rule is that the

second number divided by the first should be at least 3. So 10 x 32 is fine, just. With 8 x 32 the picture will be less magnified, but it will be brighter and wider.

**Close focusing** is another important factor. Although, obviously, binoculars are mainly for bringing distant objects closer, in fact birds occasionally hop or fly towards you, and it is a pity if you can't keep them in focus without stepping away from them. Close focus is also pretty essential if you want to look at dragonflies and butterflies through binoculars. (And you should. They look fantastic, even if you can't identify them!) Many bins these days will focus down to two or three metres (6–9 ft).

**Depth of focus** is also another important element: in practical terms, if binoculars have a small (shallow) depth of focus, you will have constantly to keep turning the focusing wheel. A greater depth means less finger work and a fuller picture.

To be honest, I could ramble on for ages about binoculars (most birdwatchers do!) but I think it would be more useful to simply list a few warnings.

**Very small binoculars,** like glorified opera glasses. Yes, you can slip them into a pocket, and the more expensive ones may be optically impressive, *but* they will have a small field of view and shallow depth of focus. You may well find it hard to "find", follow and focus on birds in the field, especially birds in flight.

**Big magnification:** It's definitely not a case of the bigger the better. Anything over 10 may be heavy and hard to hold steady, and may also have a narrow field of view, dull picture and poor close focusing.

These points will become so much clearer if you can go to that specialist and try out lots of kinds. Mind you, standards are so high these days that you may well feel there are several pairs that seem equally impressive. What's more, you may find it hard to really see much difference between a pair that is £150 and one that is £650. So what *is* the difference (apart from 500 quid)? I'm slightly tempted to say "snob value" (and there

might be a smidgeon of truth in that). The real difference, however, is reliability and ruggedness. The £650 pair should last a lifetime and be fault free. The cheaper ones may be less waterproof (they may mist up inside if you use them in heavy rain) or the picture may noticeably deteriorate over the years.

**Conclusion.** By all means buy the best you can afford, but don't be unhappy if they are in the lower price range. There really are some relatively cheap binoculars that are very good. They are certainly the ones to get if you are not yet entirely sure about the hobby, or if you intend to be a part time, or fair weather birder! Or a serviced and guaranteed second-hand pair could be the bargain you are after. One thing is for certain: I guarantee that you will be amazed and delighted by the view you get through a good pair of binoculars. They will become one of your most treasured possessions.

## A few other points

**The carrying case:** use it to protect your binoculars "in transit" if you like, but once you are in the field you simply don't need it. Your bins should be at the ready, round your neck at all times, otherwise you will miss an awful lot of birds. I lost my case years ago!

*Left: I am simply amazed that rainguards aren't standard issue with all new binoculars. A simple device that will save you so much irritation.*

cameras, yes perhaps, but for telescopes I'm not at all sure. I suppose I'd suggest you wait and see if you feel the need for them, and, if you can afford them, by all means try them. Actually, that brings me to my final conclusion on telescopes. If you can't afford one, don't worry – in many cases, if there are other birders around, they will let you have a squint through theirs! – but if you do decide to stretch the budget, you won't regret it.

Right: *Using hide clamp. Certainly simpler than wrestling with a tripod in a hide.*

Below: *How many thousand pounds worth of optical equipment, all to look at one little bird?*

## Outdoor clothing

**Coats and jackets**: Aha, the dreaded anorak! Many bird books and articles (I confess, including some of mine) adopt a rather patronising tone about "wearing something dull and rustle-free so that it doesn't scare the birds". Own up, only a bit of a twit would march out to go birding in a fluorescent orange kaghoul (not that I haven't seen it happen). Suffice it to say that you may well be out in inclement conditions and you should dress accordingly. Ironically and perversely, the best birding is often caused by bad weather: storms, rainshowers,

strong winds, fog, all sometimes ground migrant birds or blow them off course. You may find yourself miles from shelter, or even out on an open boat. Unfortunately, yachting and skiing-type gear does tend to come in lurid colours and noisy material – bird scaring costumes indeed. Hence the growth of specialist companies manufacturing clothing for outdoor pursuits – meaning nature study in general and birding in particular.

Probably birders take as much time and trouble over, and as many words have been written about, waterproof jackets as about binoculars and field guides. I'll keep it brief! The problem is that it is not so easy to road (or field) test waterproofs as optics. Maybe the shops should have showers you could dive under, or fridges you could leap into. Failing that, at least you should make sure you ask the right questions, and watch out for evasive or ambiguous answers!

Is it really waterproof? A jacket may well be marked: "windproof", "shower proof", "weather proof", etc. Most of these are euphemisms for "let's be honest, it leaks". In my experience, some of the ones that say "waterproof" also leak. The danger points are shoulders, seams and particularly pockets. In fact, I have been astonished and disappointed how many coats I've had that – despite having apparently weathered a downpour – have still left me with damp pockets, and a consequently soggy

*Left: Winter plumage. Woolly hat, which doesn't cover my ears – so that I can still hear the birds – my faithful fleece, and a small backpack containing light waterproof trousers, small telescope, and, very importantly, lunch.*

note-book and mouldy Mars bar. So grill that dealer. Make them swear their coat is totally waterproof, and take it back if it isn't.

Talking of pockets, the other requirement of good birding garments is that they have plenty of pockets. Enough to carry small books, wallet, keys, gloves, maps, emergency rations, etc, etc. Remember also that you will be wearing binoculars round your neck, so beware of voluminous collars that get in the way.

Chances are you will end up with a coat (call it an anorak if you like, but the dealer probably won't!) in some kind of guaranteed waterproof and yet breathable material (possibly lined with something ending in "ex").

You may consider getting **waterproof trousers** in the same material. Personally, I find these a bit too hot on my legs, and I tend to carry a pair of lightweight slip overs instead. In fact, especially in cold weather, most birders would agree that the "layers" principle gives you the most options. You can always take things off and tie them round your waist or stuff 'em in a bag.

Above: *Essential supplies: food, books, various contraptions: you can never have too many pockets.*

Right: *Footwear. Thank heavens for soft, lightweight boots. For years I crippled myself by wearing heavy-duty clodhoppers or wellies.*

**Boots**: again, check the waterproofing claims (you are likely to splash through somewhere soggy eventually). In my experience, the "ex" linings work well at first, but do get less efficient after a while. Wellies are fine, but can be chilly on cold days or stuffy on hot ones, and you'll get foot sore if you walk too far in them. In summer in recent years I have taken to bare feet and open sandals, and learnt to enjoy the dew between my toes!

**Hats**: by all means, but don't forget that earflaps or hoods will block out the bird song and you'll miss things that way.

If you wear glasses, you'll find a peak invaluable for keeping the rain off. I have an inexhaustible supply of baseball caps!

**Gloves**: if it's not too chilly, I prefer the fingerless type, or my "convertibles", which have a Velchro'd mitten attachment. Be honest, they've thought of most things.

**And in drier weather** …
If it's dry but chilly, I admit I am pretty much addicted to my fleece. It's got several pockets, and in fact it's waterproof enough to easily withstand anything but a real deluge. In summer, my favourite "specialist" garment is a light waistcoat with masses of pockets (like photographers often wear) but with a collar, which prevents neck chafing from binocular straps. If it's too hot even for my waistcoat – shorts weather – it's a shirt with a breast pocket for my note-book, and a "bumbag" for the other bits and pieces.

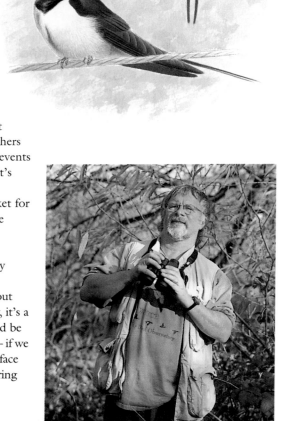

Choosing the ideal outdoor clothing may involve hours – nay years – of fun and frustration, but you will eventually sort out what you feel comfortable in. Ultimately, it's a personal thing and – be honest – it would be pretty boring – in fact, positively creepy! – if we all wore the same gear. In any case, let's face it, in the long run whatever you are wearing isn't likely to really affect what you see!

Right: *I'd not be parted from my photographers' (or birdwatchers') waistcoat, with its veritable plethora of pockets.*

capturing the shape, stance and character of a bird (what birdwatchers call the "jizz"). So – and I'm flying somewhat in the face of the accepted "notes and sketches" method here – I am going to accept what I believe is the truth: that most IDs are done by eye, rather than by deduction.

## Learning to look

So, the first vital step towards a skill in identifying birds is to train yourself to really see. Look at a bird. Take it in. Don't go rummaging through the book immediately (you may look up, and the bird will have flown away). Look, and ask yourself questions. What does this bird really look like? How big is it? Compare it with something you know. Is it the size of a House Sparrow, a Starling, a Blackbird or a goose? What shape is it? Again make comparisons. What colour or colours are there? Where are the most obvious markings? All this will help you retain a full mental picture. Then ask yourself some more questions. What kind of place is it in? Hopping on a lawn? Perching on a branch? Splashing in a pond? If it was flying was it flapping or soaring? What time of year was it?

Right: *Magpie. Surely one of the birds that really can't be mistaken for anything else?*

What part of the country, and what type of countryside? (I'll tell you why all this could be relevant in a moment.) I am not suggesting that you methodically go through a conscious checklist of such questions, but just train yourself to look and think this way. It will all help make that bird stick in your mind. Let's face it, probably the most useful attribute a potential birdwatcher could have would be a photographic memory. Or let's call it accurate visual recall. All you have to do is match the picture in your mind's eye with the one in the book.

As it happens, I truly believe that most identifications are indeed done this way – purely visually – and that – and be encouraged by this – an awful lot of them are right! Try this: work through the pages of your field guide, and mentally tick off the birds you know. Add to those the ones that

are surely unmistakable. By the time you get to the end I'm willing to bet that those 200 and odd species won't seem quite so intimidating.

## It's not in the book

The problems and puzzles arise, of course, when you see a bird that you simply can't find in the book. There could be plenty of reasons for this. Most commonly it's probably because you just didn't see it quite as well as perhaps you thought, or that your

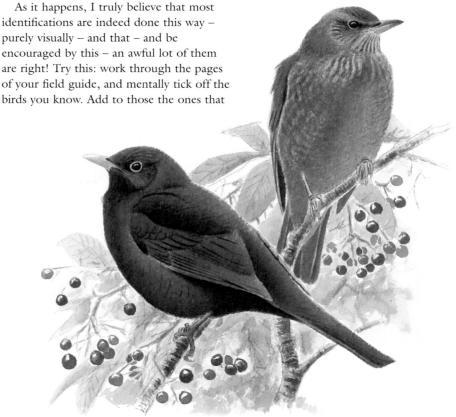

recall isn't quite accurate enough. The first – harsh – lesson of birding is: there will be birds that "get away". The consolation is that it is more than likely that you will see the species again, probably better, and next time you will be able to identify it. You may well find yourself thinking back and muttering "Ah, so that's what that was!"

There are several points to bear in mind if you see a puzzling bird. Firstly – overwhelmingly – the chances are that the bird you saw is in the book, even if you can't immediately find it. I have known many examples of this. People have come up to me and said "I've seen this funny bird. It's not in the book." But it was. Maybe not in quite the pose, or position, or plumage that they saw it, but it was there. And talking of plumage, the next vital thing to appreciate is that many species occur in a variety of plumages. Some don't – so that's a relief. Magpies, Jays, Herons, many of the

Left: *Blackbird. Well, at least the name helps ... so long as it's an adult male. Females are brown, and the young birds can look almost orangey and quite speckled.*

Right: *Chaffinch. A classic case of brightly coloured male, dowdy brown female. A rule that applies to an awful lot of birds. Unfortunately, they are not always in pairs like this.*

*Below: Herring Gull in three different plumages. Adult at the back, juvenile at the front, and 'in between' (second-year) in the middle, in sort of 'half and half' plumage. A beginner could be forgiven for thinking that these were three different species.*

geese, all basically look much the same, whatever their age or sex or time of the year (apart from the really tiny babies). Generally, when a species does have different plumages it will be the adult males that are most colourful and/or easiest to recognize. As a rule, the female will be a dowdier version of the male. She may even show some of the same markings, but much more subdued. But male and female will still be the same size and shape and share the same habits and habitat.

The most confusing and challenging birds to identify are the species that have lots of different plumages according to sex (male, female), age (adult and juveniles), and time of the year (summer and winter). It would be pretty meaningless – and arguably irritating – for me to go through lots of examples here.

sketch or take a description if you like (more of that on page 52), but you probably won't! Try to find it in the book. When you think you have found it, read the text, and as a little fail-safe double check that the bird "should" occur where and when you saw it.

You really will be encouraged by how many birds you can sort out. Of course there will always be puzzles. ID is a process of elimination. When all else fails, go through and say what it isn't!

Below: *Robin singing at night. We assume that they are inspired – fooled, more like – by street lamps or a very bright moon. I have a local bird that never seems to stop singing: does it ever sleep? Surely it must drop off sometime? Off the branch, with exhaustion, probably.*

# Mystery birds

If you *still* can't find the mystery bird in the book, there are other possibilities to consider. It could of course be a genuine rarity. In fact, this is probably the *last* thing to consider. It may seem a truism, but never forget that rarities are rare. Many experienced birders go through life without ever finding a genuine rarity for themselves. You should be so lucky as to find one (but you might be!) But first, consider other possibilities such as: is it an "aberrant", the scientific word for an unusual plumage, such as an albino (white Blackbirds and pied crows are surprisingly common), or a leucistic form (washed out biscuit colour). Or is it an escape? There are lots of birds in collections,

Left: *Rose-ringed (Ring-necked) Parakeet. Originally 'escapes', this species has become an honorary British Citizen in southeast England. A good example of another general rule: pretty birds often make horrible noises.*

Above: *Red-breasted Goose and Snow Goose. Both species occur as genuine wild rarities, but the vast majority have escaped from wildfowl collections. They are still worth looking at, though.*

cages and zoos, and they do get out and get misidentified, or at least puzzle birders and public alike. These can be anything from exotic finches to weird waterfowl. Or is it a hybrid? Ducks and geese of different species are prone to getting together and producing offspring that look either like a cross between two species or something completely different.

But hang on … what was that other life and birding rule? Don't panic! There really aren't all these weird-looking birds out there to confuse you. Never forget that the vast majority of birds are not that difficult to identify. And they *are* in the book! And the more you birdwatch, the easier you will find it to sort them out, and the fewer there will be that you can't. And it's ever such fun, anyway!

Above: *The perfect contradiction in terms: a white Blackbird. Partial albinos (those with a few white feathers) of several species are surprisingly common.*

Right: *Yellow-billed Cuckoo. A genuine rarity. I was once lucky enough to find one in late September in Dorset. It should have been in North America (where it breeds) or South America (where it winters). It may well have hitched a lift on a transatlantic liner, but it was certainly a wild bird.*

# NOTES AND LISTS

Just about every "how to watch birds" book (including some of my own) will suggest you carry a little note-book. In it, you are exhorted to record your observations in the field. Note the date, the place, the weather, the wind direction, list all the birds you see, and in particular take notes on birds you can't identify, and do drawings – field sketches – of them, noting the markings and areas of colour. Ideally, you will begin to use the topography maps and mark in the feather areas with their proper scientific names: "yellow wingbar on greater coverts, white supercilium" and so on.

Well, all this is fine. But you don't have to do it! It does sometimes bother me that this kind of detailed instruction can put off potential birdwatchers. At the very least, I've heard people plead "but I can't draw". It doesn't matter. It is perfectly possible to watch, enjoy and even identify birds without taking or keeping notes.

Having said that, note-books can be very useful and satisfying. I have two kinds: my field note-books, and my "big" note-books. The former is a little "policeman's note-book", with an attached pencil. And yes, I do jot down dates, weather, numbers of birds I see and – if necessary – the odd description and field sketch. And, if I'm lucky enough to see a bird I don't recognize, my notes and drawings may well help me to identify it. It has been said that the worst drawing is worth a page full of words, and there is some truth in that. I have a birder friend who is certainly no artist. As he put it: "I do thumbnail sketches." And as I commented: "Well they look more like thumbnails than birds!" But they have helped him sort out quite a few rarities over the years.

Sketching and note-taking are good and useful habits to get into, but in recent years I have increasingly noticed that by no means all birders do it. And that is fine. Nevertheless, I would recommend note-taking but, as it happens, not so much as an aid to identification, but as a sort of diary from which you may well get a lot of pleasure. After all my birding trips – be they a morning on Hampstead Heath or a week abroad – I write up my big note-book. Over the years, I have added sketches, paintings, photos, graphs, and indeed the odd anecdote that had very little to do with birds at all. I have books going back 40 odd years to when I started birding as a kid. They are amongst my most treasured possessions, one of the first things I would rescue if the house caught fire! And it is not just because I plunder them for books and articles. I love browsing back, remembering, reminiscing, and comparing facts and figures over the years. Exactly what form your bird diary takes is, of course, entirely up to you, but I really do recommend that you keep one.

## Lists

Another thing I would recommend keeping is a few lists. Nearly all birders do. Probably your most cherished is your UK life list (all the species you have seen in Britain, ever). You may have also a world list

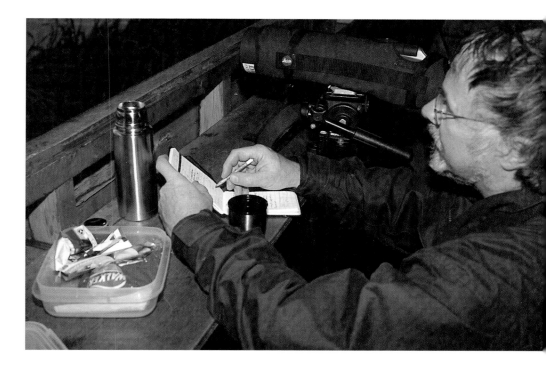

(everywhere, ever) or various holiday or trip lists. Listing can become something of an obsession  but, in any event, I do believe that list-keeping helps focus your birdwatching. You become aware of what you have learned to identify, what you've seen, and what you haven't. And it gives you incentives: what you'd like to see! To my mind, the potentially most satisfying and personal list is your local patch list.

Keeping a local list also allows you to experience a little of the thrill of rarity finding. I guarantee that every new bird you add will give you a bit of a frisson (that's a nice feeling!). What's more, there may be birds that are common elsewhere but not on your patch. For example, as a teenager,

*Above: Making field notes. Personally, I use a 'policeman's notebook', with a little pencil attached. I always have it in my pocket, and find it equally useful for jotting down shopping lists and reminders.*

week after week, I used to visit a rather desolate concrete reservoir just outside Birmingham. I will never forget my joy one Sunday morning when I found a single Coot there. Coots are, of course, common enough on most park ponds, but, for some strange reason, they were not attracted to my reservoir (can't blame 'em really: it was very bleak). In fact, this was not only the first Coot that I'd seen there, but it also turned out to be the first one recorded there for ten years. A rarity indeed.

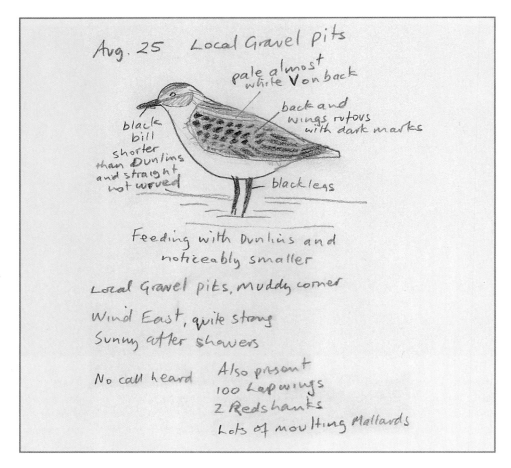

Aug. 25   Local Gravel pits

pale almost white V on back

black bill

back and wings rufous with dark marks

shorter than Dunlins and straight not curved

black legs

Feeding with Dunlins and noticeably smaller

Local Gravel pits, muddy corner

Wind East, quite strong
Sunny after showers

No call heard

Also present
100 Lapwings
2 Redshanks
Lots of moulting Mallards

## Keeping Notes

These drawings aren't exactly works of art, but if you're thinking "they're a lot better than I could do!" then don't be intimidated. They probably started out as scribbles – field sketches – done whilst watching the actual birds and the observer has then worked on them a bit before this final version went into their big notebook. In fact, he or she has noted quite enough to make positive identifications.

In both cases he or she has made a comparison with a familiar species: Dunlin and Chaffinch. If you look those up in a field guide there's a good chance that the two mystery birds will be close by, possibly even on the same or an adjacent page.

The wader is in fact a Little Stint. This is one of only two regular British waders of a similar shape, but smaller than a Dunlin and one of them (Temmink's Stint) is pretty rare. There's a good rule: always start by

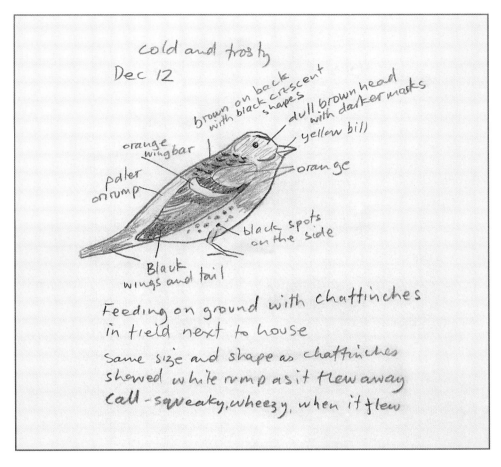

cold and frosty

Dec 12

brown on back
with black crescent
shapes

dull brown head
with darker marks

yellow bill)

orange
wingbar

paler
on rump

orange

black spots
on the side

Black
wings and tail

Feeding on ground with chaffinches
in field next to house
same size and shape as chaffinches
showed white rump as it flew away
call - squeaky, wheezy, when it flew

assuming it's the common one! The clincher here is the white 'braces' – diagnostic of Little Stint.

The finch is a Brambling (lovely name). It is sometimes referred to as the 'winter Chaffinch' and it probably will be next to it in the field guide. The white rump is a key feature, as is the wheezy call.

In both cases the date adds useful circumstantial evidence. Autumn is the time when most Little Stints pass through Britain (they don't breed here). It would be much rarer to see it in spring or winter. Conversely, a Brambling in anything but wintry months would be far less likely (they don't breed in Britain either, except very rarely in the far north).

It is also a good idea to note the weather and especially the wind direction. The east wind often brings good birds. It'd be worth nipping back to the gravel pits tomorrow to see if any more waders have arrived!

# BIRD BEHAVIOUR

I t is sometimes said – rather snobbishly perhaps – that "birders" are into ID and listing, whilst "ornithologists" study behaviour. It is true that some heavy birders – those hard-core twitchers certainly – do rarely get past identification as their main interest and concern (and believe me, it is a very elaborate study), whilst – ironically – people who may not consider themselves birders (let alone ornithologists) but simply enjoy feeding birds in the garden actually notice and may even know more about behaviour.

I'm certainly not saying that studying behaviour is a more noble pursuit, but it is endlessly absorbing. It is certainly something that will add immeasurably to your enjoyment of your local patch, and it is also on your local patch that you are most likely to notice behaviour.

Below: *Black Grouse lekking in Scotland.*
*A spectacular communal display: males showing off to the usually not-very-impressed females.*
*Even if you don't live in Scotland, you won't have to go far to see some pretty intriguing action.*

## Robins – for example

Just as an example, take some of the aspects of the lifestyle of a Robin (which is hardly an identification challenge!)

In winter, you may simply see a single bird, and hear it singing occasionally. Notice how the song is rather wistful. Then, as spring approaches, so too may other Robins. Some may be rival males. Robins are highly territorial and will defend their patch vehemently. Fights may occur. You may feel that you want to rush out and break them up. They are unlikely to be fatal encounters, but I guarantee you will be fascinated watching them. Now, the male's song becomes richer and more seductive to attract a mate. The pairs will form and there will be display, both birds sometimes bowing and wing trembling. You may be lucky enough to see them mate. Next comes choosing a nest site. Robins are almost legendary for nesting in bizarre places. You may well have provided custom-built nest boxes, but they are just as likely to choose a discarded kettle, or the window sill of an outside toilet. Then there is the period of incubation – do both male and female take turns on the eggs? Or does the male have his work cut out fending off potential egg thieves such as squirrels, Magpies and Jays? Sometimes there are tragedies: eggs are stolen or destroyed, or maybe one of the parents is killed by next door's – or even your own – cat. Or there is unseasonably cold weather, and the eggs chill and addle. All being well, they do hatch and you are treated to the frenzy of parents bringing

food back to youngsters. Some – rarely all – will fledge and leave the nest. This is the only – brief – time that fully grown Robins don't have red breasts. They are speckled, rather like tiny thrushes. You may see them cowering deep in the shade, hiding from predators, still being fed by the parents. Soon the red breasts will develop and the youngsters gain the confidence and agility to fend for themselves. By this stage, the adults are looking a right old mess, feathers broken and worn from the rigours of raising a family. They often disappear for a while in mid-summer. In fact, they are probably lying low while they moult their feathers, reappearing in early autumn looking spruce and neat again. They will probably stick around, but it is possible that, in later autumn, more Robins may appear in your garden. They could be wandering neighbours, or they could literally be foreigners. Some years there is a huge influx of continental Robins from Europe and you can actually see the difference: they tend to

Right: *In the case of most species, it's only the males that get carried away displaying, but both male and female Robins often face each other, bowing and trembling their wings. Fledgling Robins do a similar movement when they are 'begging' for their parents to feed them, so maybe this is the amorous adults' version of romantic 'baby talk'? (Scientists tell us that the titbits given by the male to the female allow her to assess how good he will be at finding food for their nestlings, help to reinforce the bond between the two birds, and provide the extra food needed by her to make the eggs.)*

Right: *Robin nesting. Actually, this one is a bit unadventurous, by Robin standards, as they are brilliantly inventive at finding quirky nest sites.*

Left: *Fighting Robins. Ironically, what we think of as one of our sweetest and most charming birds is also one of the most belligerent, though they rarely do each other serious injury. In fact, the female is testing the male to see if it's a good food finder and would, therefore, make a good mate and father.*

be greyer, with paler orange breasts and also shier than the bold Brits. They have usually moved on by early winter leaving "your" original bird, still patrolling his territory and singing wistfully, sometimes even by street lamplight on milder evenings (let's face it, that Nightingale in Berkeley Square was most likely a Robin).

OK, that was just a brief resume of a Robin's year, all observable from your kitchen window. I recount it only to illustrate how much is going on out there. Different species have different lifestyles, and they are all fascinating. The complexity and allure of bird behaviour is testified to by the number of books there are devoted to a single species or family. It is an inexhaustible study, and you can get involved in and absorbed by it without even leaving your own garden, let alone your local patch.

*Below: Robin feeding its young. This is the time when young birds are most in danger, as they may barely be able to fly. Fortunately, they are well camouflaged and pretty good at hiding. The red breast feathers will soon begin to 'sprout' amongst the speckles.*

## More than just names

I suppose what I'm driving at is that identification really is only a part of the fascination and appeal of birds and birding. Behaviour is another aspect. But it is rewarding not simply as a "scientific" study, but because it is dramatic and intriguing.

When I did *Bird in the Nest* some years ago for the BBC (in which we showed the daily goings on inside the nests of various familiar birds) someone christened it "an avian soap opera". Indeed it attracted soap opera viewing figures (up to eight million people tuned in to watch). Its attraction was clearly well beyond just birdwatchers. So what was the appeal? Well, I am pretty sure it was "behaviour", as well as an involvement with birds as individuals.

The nation collectively wept when our baby Kingfishers died.

I must admit that *Bird in the Nest* brought home to me the undeniable fact that people really do get involved with what they often think of as 'their' birds. I'm sure many of you – as I do – talk of "our Robins" or "our Blackbirds", that comfortingly establish themselves each spring, setting up their homes next to ours, in the garden or backyard. Alas, to be honest, small birds rarely live for more than a few years, so it is unlikely to be the same individuals that return for more than, say, two or three seasons. On the other hand, though the birds may change, the attractiveness of the nest sites probably doesn't, which is why – with any luck – they will be used year after year by different generations. To our eyes, the birds look identical, which is why we human beings come to think of them as 'our birds', friends almost. We literally become involved in their lives. Now, I have heard 'heavy' birders, or serious ornithologists, dismissing this attitude as soppy and sentimental. Well, all I can say to that is that I am one of the soppiest. What's more, observing and getting involved with the daily lives of birds may be sentimental, but it is surely also the very essence of studying bird behaviour. The science of ... yes, ornithology. You may be more of a scientist than you realized.

I also think that a large part of the appeal of watching birds and their behaviour is

Left: *Kingfisher. Undeniably beautiful. Whether sitting still on a branch, watching and waiting, or plunging into the water in search of a fish, they are fascinating to watch.*

Left: *Very young Great Tits with no feathers yet and eyes barely open.*

Below: *Blue Tits already almost fully feathered, being fed by mother.*

purely aesthetic. I don't just mean that birds are beautiful, or charming or cute or impressive – though different species are all these things – I mean that sometimes there are moments of incredible visual action or amazing shapes. Many photographers strive to capture such moments. It may be birds displaying, fighting, preening and contorting, flying or flocking. The picture will be affected by the angle, the view, the weather, the lighting conditions – all the things that add up to an unforgettable image. Photographers try to freeze the moment. You – as a birder – should search out such images and try to preserve them in your mind's eye. They are the unerasable memories that will stick with you for ever. I realize that I am waxing a bit lyrical, but it's true, and I really believe that the crucial step towards noticing these things is awareness of what can happen: training your eye to look for it.

Above: *Moorhens are one of the most distinctive and easy to see waterbirds in Europe. Their bulky body and short wings mean that flight is difficult.*

Left: *Adult moorhens are good parents, taking great care of their young.*

Below: *Moorhens are highly territorial birds and fights are commonplace.*

Above: *Large flocks of Woodpigeons are a common sight as they leave trees or fields.*

Below: *Woodpigeons feeding in a field of cut corn. Scarecrows and other deterrents won't keep them away.*

# SONGS AND CALLS

This is possibly the area that intimidates beginners more than any other. I won't exactly alleviate any concern by stating that I reckon well over 50 per cent of the birds that I see, I actually first locate or mainly identify by the noises they make. So, yup, I can't deny it, it is ever so useful to get to know bird song and bird calls. With no due modesty at all, I'd claim to be pretty good at it. Whenever I do radio interviews it seems the host tries to catch me out (show me up?) by playing to me bird CDs and challenging me to identify them. So far I've managed to get them all. As it happens, none of them have been that difficult, but nevertheless the interviewer has been appropriately and satisfyingly impressed. So how is it done? My only answer is: "experience". And frankly, that is the secret, i.e. there really is no secret. So no short cuts here.

How do you acquire this skill? OK, the first step: when you are out – listen! Any bird noise you don't recognize, try to see what is making it. Connect the sound to the sight. Next time, hopefully, you will recognize it. If not, try again. Keep doing it. It'll come. Eventually. Honest. But don't worry if it is a slow process, and rest assured that even the most efficient aural expert will hear something now and again that he or

Below: *Sky Lark and its sonogram. Justly famous for its 'never ending' song, which you can often hear even though the bird is so high in the sky that it is invisible to the naked eye.*

Right: *Cupping ears to help locate birdsong. I know it looks a bit daft, but you really can hear soft or distant noises much more clearly by doing this.*

Above right: *One way of learning songs is to record them on a cassette or mini disc. Playing them back may attract the bird closer, but don't overdo it as the poor bird may get a bit frantic, and indeed frustrated, when it cannot see the rival that is actually only a recording.*

# Noises draw attention

Why learn birdsong? Well, there are several reasons. A bird may be hidden in bushes, woodland, or reeds; the only way you may even know it is there is its song. Your attention may be drawn to birds flying way up overhead, for example, wild geese calling.

Distress calls may lead you to other birds. For example, crows cawing or gulls screeching as they mob a large bird of prey. Blackbirds and other small birds giving alarm calls and "scolding" may be because they have discovered a roosting owl. So may you!

*Below: A Stonechat and Meadow Pipits 'mobbing' a Short-eared Owl that probably just wanted a nap. Mind you, Short-eared Owls do often hunt by day, so maybe the smaller birds are right not to trust it.*

*Above: A Red Kite gliding silently overhead would be easy to miss if it weren't for the frantic cawing of the crows 'seeing it off'.*

**67**

# Identification

This especially applies in the UK, where we have several species that look so similar (often the notorious "little brown jobs") that they are best identified by song or call. For example, Chiffchaff and Willow Warbler look almost identical (see pages 16-17), but have totally different songs. Indeed, the Chiffchaff was named after its monotonous song – "chiff-chaff" – whilst the Willow Warbler has a lovely, wistful, cascading song. They could hardly sound more different.

Wild geese and waders are two other families within which several species look very similar. The calls are the easiest way to tell them apart, and are, in fact, quite often the reason that you noticed the birds in the first place, as they often fly above or away from you. Wild geese and waders often look very much the same, and the calls are the easiest way to tell them apart.

You should trust your field guide to point out when a call or song is important and indeed in some cases how to listen for them.

Above: *Green Sandpiper (above) and Wood Sandpiper (below). These two look very similar, but their calls are completely different. Wood calls "chif-if-if", whilst Green Sandpiper utters a liquid, rather panicky-sounding "tweet weet weet!", which may not look very distinctive written down, but is when you hear it.*

## Aesthetic

The final reason for becoming aware of bird noises is surely aesthetic. Quite simply, bird song can be absolutely delightful, and the calls can be incredibly atmospheric.

The person who coined the phrase "silent spring" to encapsulate the potential horror of losing our song birds to persecution and pollution surely got it spot on. Imagine a world without bird songs and calls. A sad place indeed.

Finally, take heart if you are still feeling apprehensive about sorting it all out. Believe me, I know experienced birders whose visual identification skills are impressive, but who confess to having a blind spot – or rather a deaf ear – when it comes to sorting out calls and songs. But they still manage to be pretty good birders. Nevertheless, they don't simply ignore bird songs and calls, and neither should you. Just enjoy the sound – even if you don't know what's making it. But I bet you'll want to find out!

Left: *People often rave about the dawn chorus, but there is another burst of song just before sundown. This dusk chorus can be just as impressive, and you don't have to get up early to hear it.*

# FINDING BIRDS

Now of course – again – you don't *have* to do this, but I personally find the most consistently absorbing type of birding is visiting and watching the same place over a long period. You really do get to know it and its birds. It's not just a matter of ticking them off or seeing how many you can record. It's

getting to know how they vary over the year, where they nest, what appears only in winter, what in summer, when the migrants arrive, when they leave. Noticing their habits, displays, behaviour in general, and indeed recognizing and studying individual birds. I suppose in some ways the most intense local patch watcher is the person who simply feeds, watches and gets to know and love the birds in their own backyard. Probably people who wouldn't call themselves birdwatchers at all!

Top: *Tottenham Marshes. A mixture of habitats in a small area is an ideal 'local patch'.*
Above: *River habitat. River valleys often act as avian motorways for migrating birds.*

Right: *Great Crested Grebe. Now common over much of Britain, thanks to bird protection laws and lots of flooded gravel pits and reservoirs. A delight to birdwatchers and non-birdwatchers.*

## Your local patch

Indeed, your own backyard or garden may well be your local patch, but birdwatchers generally choose something a little more elaborate. My own patch is Hampstead Heath, and it fulfills the criteria pretty well. It has a mixed variety of habitats – woodland, hedges, open fields, some areas of water, and even a small reedbed. Also – and perhaps most exciting to me – it has Parliament Hill, which overlooks London and seems to lie on some kind of migration route, so that in spring and autumn the birding can vary greatly from day to day, as warblers, swallows and martins, pipits, thrushes, etc pass through or over on their various migratory journeys. Every now and then I see a local rarity – remember anything that is new for your local patch is rare – but the greatest satisfaction is in keeping a record over the years and realizing that no two years are ever the same. There are certainly more productive patches than the Heath (and some less so as well, I imagine) but wherever you live you can bet there will be somewhere worth watching. A park, allotments, a stretch of canal – even or indeed especially in an urban area – a local reservoir or gravel pits, a river valley in suburbia or in the country, right up to an estuary, headland or island on the coast. I don't want to go on about it, but I really do think that any birdwatcher who hasn't done at least a bit of "patch work" has really missed something.

## Finding your own birds – where to look and when

One of the most valuable skills – or is it an instinct? – that a birdwatcher can possess is recognizing a good bird place. Of course, experience is the key to it all. It's something you will inevitably practise on a relatively small scale on your local patch. For example, I recall even on my very first visit to Hampstead Heath, I could anticipate which areas certain birds would prefer. Most obviously, I would expect wildfowl on the ponds, but even within these areas there were preferences. The deeper open water for diving ducks, like Tufted and Pochard; the shallower edges for dabblers, like Mallard; the shady banks for Moorhens, and so on. Where there are overhanging branches and a few reeds, that's where I'd expect Great Crested Grebes to nest – and they do. In fact, knowing what you expect (or at least hope) to see in a certain type of habitat is the very essence of efficient birdwatching. Wherever you go, you should be thinking: "What kind of birds like this kind of habitat?" You should almost assume that they are there somewhere, and make a point of trying to find them. Back on the Heath, for example, I would search the mature woodland trees for woodpeckers, Treecreepers, Nuthatches and tits – and most days that's exactly where I find them.

Left: *Each bird in its place. Whinchat and Red-backed Shrike on isolated perches. Wheatears hopping on the rocks, Hobby in the air. They are on real heath here, but I have seen them all at Hampstead Heath, almost in the middle of London.*

The hedgerows are more favoured by Blackbirds, Song Thrushes and Dunnocks, and in summer by warblers such as Whitethroats and Blackcaps. On the short grassed playing fields, I'd expect gulls in winter, especially if the ground has become soggy. In spring and autumn the same fields may attract migrant Wheatears or pipits, while on the scattered perches of dock or thistles I'd look for Whinchats or Stonechats. Neither are common in Hampstead, but when they do occur I can accurately predict where they will be.

But few – perhaps no – birdwatchers can live on their local patch alone. You will inevitably want to go travelling and seek out new places and new birds. The principle, however, is the same – certain types of habitat or terrain will attract particular types of birds, and wherever you visit, you should be aware of what you "expect" to see.

*Above: Urban allotments. As well as breeding birds, migrants often use allotments to 'refuel'. They can be particularly lively places during spring and autumn migration.*

Fortunately, these days there are masses of excellent books available on "where to watch birds" either in Britain and Ireland, or much more locally. Nearly all regions or counties have a "where to watch" guide. So buy these, read them, choose your locations, and prepare for the trip by checking on the area's specialities. The text of a good field guide will also keep reminding you of each species' habitat preferences.

All I am going to do here is list a variety of some of the more productive habitats, with a few notes on birding techniques, which I hope will help you make the most of your visit. It may also help you to recognize potentially good bird areas when you are exploring for yourself.

# In town

It is a total fallacy to assume that there aren't many birds in urban areas. The very fact that there so much is built up means that bird-friendly oases act as magnets. It is probably easier to anticipate the good places in town than it is in the countryside. It is certainly easier to define and decide on a local patch in or near urban areas. Try gardens, especially those with a good variety of native trees and shrubs. Parks, especially those with lakes, and particularly if there is a dog and people-free area, possibly fenced off and designated as an urban nature reserve. Also allotments and cemeteries. Canals and river banks not only attract waterbirds but also often act as migration routes for small birds, as do high places, such as Parliament Hill near where I live in London. These can

be fantastic viewpoints for visible migration. Keep looking up! It's amazing how many birds fly high – often unnoticed – over towns and cities. You can see everything from Cormorants and geese to migrating swallows, martins and Swifts. Swifts of course actually prefer buildings to nest in, as do Kestrels and Pied Wagtails. There is also

Below: *Kestrel. Another bird that is happy on the artificial cliff faces and ledges of buildings.*

Bottom: *Black Redstart. On the Continent, they breed in rocky terrain. Derelict sites, power stations and warehouses are their British home.*

Left: *Swifts in flight. The 'screaming' of Swifts is one of the characteristic sounds of summer, and is a wild noise over the middle of a city. They usually arrive in early May to nest under the roofs of houses.*

an increasing number of rooftop gull colonies, even in totally landlocked cities, and – ironically perhaps – rubbish tips attract huge numbers of gulls and gull watchers. Many of Britain's rarest gulls have been recorded on "dumps". British Black Redstarts after the Second World War became addicted to bomb sites and they still prefer derelict urban areas.

Left: *Walthamstow Reservoir. A concrete reservoir much like the one that I studied when I was a lad. Definitely most productive in winter.*

Below: *Flooded gravel pit. Many gravel companies work with local wildlife trusts to create nature reserves when the pits are no longer in operation.*

## Gravel pits and reservoirs

Probably the favourite local patches amongst birders and they are possibly the most birded type of habitat overall. They are good value since they not only attract the expected water birds, but also seem to act as a magnet to passing migrants in spring and autumn. Moreover, the bird population will change with the seasons. The bleaker waters tend to be at their best during the winter, when ducks flock together and there is an influx of extra birds from the continent. More sheltered areas – particularly disused gravel pits – especially if they have reedbeds,

Above: *An east wind and thundery weather in May. Ideal conditions for Black Terns – probably on their way to breed in Holland – to get 'displaced' over British reservoirs. They may stay for only a few minutes, so you have to be there at the right time.*

tend to be at their most entertaining during spring, summer and autumn, with the additional attractions of dragonflies and aquatic plants and flowers. The fact is though that such areas offer all-year value. Two tips: a telescope is definitely essential at a big reservoir, and do walk round till you get the sun behind you.

## Estuaries and coastal marshes

These are splendidly prolific areas for birds, offering such spectacles as huge flocks of wild geese in winter, or a variety of migrant waders in spring and autumn. Fortunately, nowadays a large number of such places are official nature reserves.

Mind you, the downside to that is that there are relatively few such areas left round our coasts that have not been developed and degraded. The ones that remain are havens for wildlife only because they are officially protected. But let's be grateful that they exist, and, what's more, they do offer all the viewing facilities of an official reserve. My main tips here are – yet again – get that sun behind you. Waders and wildfowl are challenging enough to sort out, without making it more difficult by squinting into the sun at them. Also, check the tide tables. Mudflats at low tide can be dauntingly vast

Left: *Knot and Dunlins, high-tide roost flock at Snettisham RSPB Reserve in north Norfolk. It's worth checking to find out which are the best tides for seeing really spectacular numbers.*

Below: *Brent Geese. Winter visitors in increasing numbers to estuaries and coastal marshes. Their distant calls sound like a huge pack of yapping dogs.*

and bleak, and indeed appear relatively birdless, but as the tide comes in birds will be concentrated in ever more densely packed flocks. If the tide gets really high, they may then fly off to inaccessible and unviewable offshore sandbanks, rocks, or saltmarshes. As the tide begins to fall, they will return to feed as soon as the first strips of mud are exposed, and this is another excellent time to see them. Flocks of waders flying to and from their roosts are amongst the world's great bird spectacles. Clouds of birds, constantly changing shape (the clouds I mean, not the birds). It seems amazing that they don't sometimes collide. And the sounds! You can literally hear the swoosh of wings as the birds wheel past or overhead. This is a good opportunity to get to know calls and wing patterns, but mainly just to enjoy the spectacle.

Below: *A typical estuary selection. Gulls, waders and wildfowl. You soon appreciate which species prefer which areas: soft mud, sand, pebbles or shallow water. Take your time to scan, and make sure you see everything that there is to see.*

## Sea cliffs and seabird islands

Once again, the fact is that there aren't that many big seabird colonies that aren't official reserves, so finding them and accessing them is easy enough. Do be aware though that cliffs that are teeming with life during the summer breeding season are literally birdless in winter. The only other note of caution I will add is: do be careful. I have seen people taking ridiculous risks leaning over precipices to get a better view. This is particularly dangerous when you are looking through binoculars or a camera, when you can easily lose your sense of how close to the edge you are.

"Where to Watch" books will tell you exactly where to go, what to expect to see and the best times to visit.

We're very lucky in the UK to have some of the best seabird spectacles in the world.

be unpleasant: wet and windy. You may well decide it's all a bit more than you can manage! My advice would be that if you happen to be at a seawatching location and there is a bunch of birders staring out to sea, ask them if there is much action. "Anything happening?" is the usual enquiry. If the answer is "yes", make yourself cozy on the end of the line, and have a go. Listen to what's being said. Someone will invariably be giving a running commentary and calling out directions. "Red-throated Diver flying past the blue buoy at 3 o'clock." The latter refers to direction, not the time! Imagine you are the centre of a clock and 12 o'clock is directly in front of you. So 3 o'clock is some way to the right. Don't be discouraged if at first you seem to miss more than you see. And don't be shy about asking. Equally, if you find it all a bit more stressful than enjoyable, don't be afraid to pack it in and try something easier! By the way, early morning tends to be the best time for seawatching, with a possible resurgence in the late afternoon, and be sure to be prepared for that unexpected squall.

## Pelagics

This is seawatching for the more adventurous, and those with a steady stomach.

The RSPB and other groups organize boat trips – for example, from Bridlington in Yorkshire or off the coast of Cornwall – which get you out where seabirds really belong – on the ocean. Beware though that this by no means guarantees that you will find many – or indeed any – birds. I'll just say that pelagics can be fantastic, or total nightmares. Either way, they are likely to be memorable so – as ever – my advice is go and try one. (You don't mind if I don't come with you though, do you?)

Left: *Pelagic birds at sea. Pelagos means sea (in Greek), and it is undeniably an exciting experience to be out there, where the birds belong, and to realize what an extraordinarily harsh life they lead.*

Below: *Seawatchers brave all weathers, so don't forget to wrap up warm!*

## Woodland

Another habitat where early morning is certainly the best time to be out, if only to enjoy the dawn chorus, undiluted by the sounds of distant traffic and aeroplanes. Woodland birds are more vocal and active in the early hours, and therefore easier to hear and see, as they are more likely to be flitting around looking for food. It is the sound that will catch your attention (this is where it really helps to get to know songs and

Right: *Garden Warbler on the edge of woodland. One of those secretive warblers that you can often hear singing from deep within a bush, but you are blowed if you can see it.*

Below: *Redwing. A winter thrush that is addicted to red berries. A flock of Redwings can strip a cotoneaster tree in no time.*

calls) and it is movement that will attract your eye. Woodland watching is inevitably easier when the air is calm and the leaves aren't rustling and shimmering. But remember, even on a windy day, leaves rarely float upwards! A bird that may be invisible in the treetops will suddenly become obvious when it flits from branch to branch (or maybe flies up and away). Also, think like a bird. The vast majority of a woodland bird's daytime activity is to do with display (including singing) or feeding. A bird in song is likely to be static and therefore hard to spot, so you need to follow your ear, as it were. On many occasions, the singer may in fact be on a fairly conspicuous perch – a bare branch or even the very top of a tree. So try scanning the likely song perches. Calling birds are more likely to be on the move, foraging for food. The calls themselves take experience to sort out (many of them are soft and very similar "tsips" and "seesees") but fortunately the movements are likely to catch your eye. And think what the birds are feeding on, and search accordingly. Trees with berries are likely to attract Blackbirds and thrushes. Insect eaters seek out sunny patches, where flies are most likely to swarm. The edge of the wood, where the sunlight hits the outer trees is the best and easiest

place to look for warblers and flycatchers. Some birds seem to be almost addicted to certain trees. Siskins and Redpolls love alders and birches. Again, a good field guide will point you in the right direction.

Woodlands can sometimes seem strangely empty. At around midday things often go very quiet, as birds rest and preen. In mid-winter the birds flock together more (for safety and efficiency of searching) and it's all too easy to fail to connect with them. Late summer can seem deadest of all, though ironically there may be more birds in the woods than at any other time. However, newly fledged youngsters are hiding from potential predators and keeping very quiet, and the adults are also keeping a low profile while they moult into fresh plumage.

Nevertheless, a good morning in a woodland can be truly magical. The secret is get up early, move slowly and quietly, and take your time. I am personally not convinced that birding in groups is the best way to work a woodland, but – having said that – dawn chorus walks are extremely popular, and I have never met any one who has been on one and didn't thoroughly enjoy it.

Left: *Mistle Thrush singing. Mistle Thrushes often start singing very early in the year – even in midwinter – almost invariably from the very top of a tall tree.*

Right: *Siskin on hazel. They also love alders and birches. Addicted to catkins? They can also be seen feeding on nut bags in your garden.*

Below: *Foraging tit flock. Other species will often tag along, including Treecreepers, Goldcrests and Nuthatches. Food finding is much more efficient in a flock, and there is safety in numbers.*

# Moorland and mountain

Exploring this kind of habitat is likely to be as much hiking and trekking as birding. It's good for you, even if you don't see much! In winter, the uplands can be literally birdless, but in summer there are certain specialities that are definitely worth searching for, be it Ptarmigan and Dotterel in the Cairngorms, Golden Eagles in the Highlands, or Ring Ouzels and Golden Plover on the moors. Be prepared for a lot of walking and possibly bad weather, and make sure you know where you are, where you're going, and how to get back. The birds may not always "perform", but now and again you will have a really memorable day out, in an atmosphere that is totally unique, and a complete contrast to, say, the teeming activity at a seabird colony, or the teeming birdwatchers at a coastal reserve!

Above: *Dotterel. Hard to find on their mountain-top breeding grounds, but, if you do, they can be delightfully tame.*

Right: *Golden Plover. On the breeding grounds you could see their parachuting display flight.*

Above right: *Ring Ouzel. Sometimes known as the 'Mountain Blackbird', its mournful song literally echoes around the ravines.*

## Other locations – and general rules

I can't stress it enough: different habitats attract different birds. Whether you are looking to add to your day list or your life list, the secret is to visit as many types of terrain as possible, not only those I have already suggested. There are others that have their specialities: for example, the ancient conifer forests of Scotland for Capercaillie, Crested Tit and Scottish Crossbill; the oak woods of Wales for Pied Flycatchers, Redstarts and Wood Warblers; the heathlands of Dorset for Nightjars and Dartford Warblers, and many more.

I have tried to show their magic on my TV

Below: *Crested Tit. Another one that in Britain you will find only north of the Border, and yet they also live in the southern Mediterranean region.*

especially at lakes and estuaries, so give yourself half an hour, rather than half a minute.

Mind you, my final piece of hide advice is: don't stay in there too long. The view through hide windows is often terrific, but it is also limited. You can't see what's above or behind you. I have told this salutary tale before, but it illustrates a point. I was at Minsmere one morning, walking along a path through the reedbeds, when I spotted six distant dots flying towards me from way down the coast. As they got closer I realized they were Spoonbills. To my delight, they flew right above my head and circled high over the main scrape. But they didn't land. For some reason they glided on and away, until I lost them over the horizon. Nevertheless, I'd had a terrific view, lacking only the extra pleasure of sharing it with other birders. But maybe I could. At that moment, the door of the nearby hide opened and two birdwatchers emerged. "Hey! What about those Spoonbills!?" I enthused. They looked puzzled and more than a little deflated. "Er … what Spoonbills?"

But then again that's birdwatching: you can't win 'em all.

Above: *Spoonbills flying over – a terrific view.*

Left: *Spoonbills feeding. The sort of close-up view you would probably only get from a hide. On the other hand, they may just fly straight over.*

Right: *Inside a hide. A chance to chat to other birdwatchers, of all ages and levels of expertise.*

# TWITCHING

The media now use the word "twitcher" to refer to any and all birdwatchers. This is as inaccurate as saying that all sprinters are athletes, therefore all athletes are sprinters! Strictly speaking, twitching is a very specific and somewhat extreme kind of birding. It is rarity hunting. It is also often mass birding, when crowds of hundreds, sometimes even thousands, gather at one place to tick off a rare bird that they already know has been found (and they hope is still there!) In a sense, therefore, twitching is the very antithesis of what I personally feel is the essence of birding: unpredictability, the fact that you never really know what you are going to see. If you go twitching, you know exactly what you are going to see (or at least hope you are going to see!). The fact is, it may have flown off. Arguably, this adds to the excitement, though it also means that twitching can be a frenetic and stressful activity. Indeed the derivation of the word indicates this. It was coined many years ago to describe a bunch of early twitchers who supposedly became so overexcited at the prospect of seeing a new bird, and so riddled with anxiety at the possibility of missing it, that they would literally shake, tremble or "twitch" with the emotion of the whole thing!

I'll be honest, twitching is not really my bag – as we used to say back in the sixties, when I did a bit of twitching, and proved to myself that I really couldn't stand the strain – but, I assure you, I have absolutely nothing against it. I would say that if rarity hunting becomes a total obsession, to the extent that you become oblivious to behaviour and beauty, then that's a bit sad. But I really don't think that even the most hardened twitcher is that far gone! The truth is, that most birders do a bit of twitching now and again. In fact, I would recommend that you try it.

The information technology these days is simply fantastic. You can ring Birdline (national or local) and you will hear constantly updated news of rare birds, plus instructions of how to find them. Pagers are even more amazing: they even bleep or vibrate when a mega rarity is found, and you'll get a sort of running commentary on the little screen: "the bird is showing well ... the bird hasn't been seen for half an hour, etc, etc". So, if you fancy a weekend's twitching, why not? Choose a bird, and go for it! I will simply add a few more comments.

## Disadvantages

Twitching can be expensive (on phone bills and petrol) and time-consuming. You may spend more time on the road driving than birdwatching.

You may find the big crowds positively claustrophobic (I do).

You may not see the bird (twitchers call this "dipping out") and believe me this can be pretty upsetting (I've seen twitchers in tears!).

It is arguably a bit pointless (or premature) for a beginner. I guess I'm being a rather purist, but it is surely better to get to know

*Above: Crowds of this size are common when a rare bird is reported, even if it is a boring 'little brown job'. So, do you fancy this kind of birding? I confess that my personal answer is: "Not a lot." But I'd recommend that you do go on a twitch, and make up your own mind. It's an experience!*

the commoner birds and birding techniques before going off rarity chasing. Rarities can wait. But then again can they? You may get news of an extreme rarity – a first for Britain perhaps – that may never turn up again in your lifetime, so why not go for it?

## Advantages

You are more or less guaranteed to see some "good" birds, and there is an undeniable frisson about rarities. This is enhanced by the shared experience. It is rather nice to share your joy if the bird is showing well (or your sorrow if it isn't!). In any event, the social side of twitching is – to me – arguably the most enjoyable side of it. I very rarely go twitching, but when I do I enjoy seeing friends and faces as much as the bird itself. It's certainly a consolation if the bird has flown.

What certainly is true is that twitching (in its true sense) is here to stay. So too are birdlines and pagers. So why not take advantage of them, to whatever extent you choose? For example, I ring Birdline to keep up to date with what's going on, especially in my local area. If I have seen good local migration over the Heath, I like to hear whether or not other areas in the south-east have had similar experiences. I confess I have also rung Birdline to check out where *not* to go if I want to avoid the crowds!

A phenomenon I have noticed increasingly in recent years is birdwatchers that I certainly wouldn't call heavy twitchers using Birdline or their pagers to give a shape to their weekend's birding. For example, one early October I was in north Norfolk. There was a big fall of migrant birds and a lot of possible locations to choose from. As it happens, I decided to do my own thing and try to find my own birds. However, as I

Left: *Boarding boats at St Agnes, Isles of Scilly. Chasing rarities around this rare-bird Mecca can be frustrating. You can't be on several islands at the same time, and you can, quite literally, miss the boat.*

Above: *On your marks, get set, go! Racing for a rarity? Well, twitchers have been known to leap overboard before the boat docks, and then wade – or swim! - to get there first. Honestly!*

explored the coastline, I kept meeting people who were letting their pagers dictate their itineraries. They followed the latest news up and down the coast from one rarity to another. Some they saw, some they didn't, but generally they seemed to be having a thoroughly good time, and the hit and miss element seemed to be adding to the fun rather than the frustration. I think! Personally, I'm sure I couldn't have stood the strain! What's more, the kudos and thrill of finding my own rarity and putting it on the pager appeals to my vanity. But each to his or her own. I stress again, the technology is in place, thousands of people enjoy twitching now and again, so for heaven's sake give it a try. Being a child of the seventies (well, a 30-year-old of the

seventies actually), I quote that well known hippy maxim: "whatever turns you on". I'm talking about birding of course.

I would just, however, like to repeat my grumble about the media using the word (and image) of twitching as if that is what birdwatching is all about. It's not only inaccurate, it's also potentially off-putting. I mean, I somehow can't imagine too many non-birdwatchers seeing the scene opposite and thinking: "Oh, that looks fun. I wish I were there."

# AUTUMN

## August and September

Once autumn migration gets underway, this is the season when the bird population can change literally overnight. It is worth visiting your patch day after day. The small waders with black bellies are Dunlins: all adults, which may indicate a poor breeding season, although generally the juveniles (they don't have black bellies) do travel later anyway. The Curlew-like birds (several of them snoozing) are in fact Whimbrels, which may have bred in the Northern Isles of Scotland. Perched in the foreground is a juvenile Whinchat, taking on 'fuel' before making an amazing journey down to Africa. Likewise, Swallow roosts build up in the reedbeds – sometimes, flocks may number thousands – before they finally set off south, mainly in late September. Most British Swallows spend our winter in South Africa.

# LATE AUTUMN, EARLY WINTER

## October, November and December

A nd the year comes full circle. But before that, October: many birdwatchers' favourite month. There may be a few lingering summer migrants, but this is the time when winter visitors arrive. Wildfowl include Whooper Swans, and a flock of Barnacle Geese – in ancient times people believed that they summered under the sea and hatched from barnacle shells. The single Snow Goose may be a genuine wild bird, but is just as likely to be an 'escape' that has latched onto the Barnacle flock. Redwings and Fieldfares from Scandinavia are tucking into the hawthorn berries, and, nearby, there are a couple of tiny Goldcrests and, above them, a couple of Snow Buntings. These may indicate an influx of migrants from farther east: the Continent or even beyond. They may have been blown across to Britain by an east wind. 'Falls' of migrants often include something unusual. October is the rare-bird month. Ask any twitcher!

# CONSERVATION

These days, everybody knows that birds – and other wildlife – are under threat. It is unarguable that many previously common species are diminishing in numbers. It is most obvious to someone of my age when I go for a walk in the British countryside. When I was a kid, back in the early 1950s, I did a lot of my birdwatching on farmland on the edge of Birmingham. In winter, I could expect to see flocks of Yellowhammers and Tree Sparrows, and in summer I would find Lapwings and Skylarks nesting in just about every field. If I visited the same farmland now I simply would not see those birds in such numbers. Some of them may have gone entirely. But it is not all doom and gloom. There are other species that have increased. Very often it is as a result of conservation and the management efforts of organizations such as the RSPB, the Wildlife Trusts, the Wildfowl and Wetlands Trust, English Nature, and other more local groups. In the context of this book, let me reassure you that there are still plenty of birds to watch!

Right: *Male Hobby at nest. In recent years, these lovely falcons have bred in woodland near my home in London. Like most birds of prey, they are flourishing because of stricter controls over persecution and poisoning. But I was pretty amazed to find a Hobby's nest in such an urban area.*

fir tree behind the shed, and I can hear the "si si si" of a little flock of Long-tailed Tits as they go rollicking through the willow (I have still never seen Long-tailed Tits on a feeder, but they have taken up this activity in some parts of England). In any case, the House Sparrows have just taken over. I do have five House Sparrows regularly in my garden. Alas, they are becoming quite a rarity these days. They have mysteriously almost disappeared from many of our cities. So, I am particularly pleased to see a pair with three of last year's youngsters, all looking fit and well fed. I'd like to think I've helped them through the winter.

So, that's not bad is it? Over a dozen species out there in my little garden at this very minute, and – with any luck – six or seven of them will stay on to breed. Imagine that happening in literally thousand of gardens across the country (and indeed the world!) and you can appreciate that it really is an example of conservation in practice on a very grand scale.

So, at the very least, feed the birds and put up a couple of nest boxes. But if you fancy providing something more elaborate – and even more productive – there are some excellent books (not to mention the occasional television series!) that will tell you how to create everything from ponds and marsh gardens to wildflower meadows. I can't resist saying it again: "Build it, and they will come!"

Left: *A bird-friendly garden. What a great garden! It's obviously the work of a wildlife lover with several different habitats. Don't worry if your patch is much smaller.*

Right: *Goldfinches on teasel heads. I know many gardeners hate the thistle family, but seed-eating birds love them. That's the key to good wildlife gardening: leave some of it messy. It's less work that way, too.*

# BIRDING EVENTS

I've said before that if I were challenged to turn a non-birdwatcher on to birds I would take them on a trip to the seabird colonies of the Farne Islands. If – as an extension of that – I was asked to introduce them to the whole world of birdwatching, I would take them to the Bird Fair. When I say 'the' fair, I mean the incredible event that takes place on the third weekend of August every year at Rutland Water Nature Reserve. The first one was held over ten years ago in – as I recall – a single, relatively small marquee. Nowadays, there are several massive marquees and several thousand visitors over the weekend, who come from all over the country. Many of them are, of course, already birdwatchers, but many are not. Families, children of all ages, people who are simply curious to find out what this birdwatching thing is all about, are all guaranteed a fun and fascinating time. Moreover, I am absolutely certain that they are amazed at the scale of the event.

# The Bird Fair

So what is the Bird Fair? It is a cross between a trade fair, an exhibition and a festival. I think of it also as a celebration. Every possible aspect of birds and birding is on display at stands or stalls. You can try out every binocular, telescope and item of photographic gear on the market; browse through every book; try on every type of outdoor clothing; sample the videos, CD-ROMs, computer programmes and audio tapes. In the art tent, many of the world's top wildlife illustrators display their work and, indeed, are actually painting, sculpting or wood carving before your very eyes. Travel companies from Britain and abroad are represented, as are conservation groups from a variety of countries. You can make your purchases there and then, everything from a painting, to a new binocular strap, to a three-week cruise round the Antarctic.

But it's not just about selling and buying. There is an overflowing programme of illustrated talks, lectures, demonstrations and bird-related activities for youngsters, plus fashion shows, panel games and quizzes, some of which are fairly serious, while others are extremely frivolous. There is good food, live music, and – when you feel like a break – there is excellent birdwatching on the reserve itself. Frankly, it is impossible for me to conjure up what a truly fantastic event this is. I have attended (well, been frantically involved in actually) all but one Rutland Bird Fair since its inception and they just get bigger and

*Left: Rutland Bird Fair. As you can see from the signposts, there's a lot of events: there's bound to be something for everyone.*

better. Unreservedly, I recommend you go.

But what if you are not able to get to Rutland on the third weekend of August? Don't fret. Happily, the success of Rutland has encouraged many other – admittedly smaller – but still hugely entertaining events in various parts of the country. There is a regular Birdwatching and Photographic Fair in July in the Midlands, and others in other areas of Britain. I also hear of more and more in other countries from Poland to the USA. So, wherever you live, at some point in the year, chances are you will have the opportunity to get along to a Bird Fair not too far away.

## And there's more

Also, the big conservation organizations frequently hold open days at their most popular reserves or centres, which in many ways are like mini Bird Fairs, again featuring birding products, talks, guided walks and so on.

I have mentioned the benefits of guided group birding. In fact, the RSPB and the Wildlife Trusts hold all sorts of events, which focus more specifically on particular aspects of birds or birding. For example, dawn chorus days, winter wildfowl identification, high tide wader watches, spring migrant specials, and so on and so forth. They really are terrific value, and many of them are so popular that they get booked out well in advance. Members of all such societies will get detailed programmes of events, which go on throughout the year. I cannot stress too strongly that by joining you are not only helping conservation, you are also helping yourself. You get an awful lot back in return.

# BIRDS IN CYBERSPACE

I have to confess that I am completely computer unfriendly (actually, I would claim that computers are unfriendly to me!) I do use a word processor, but any Internet searching or emailing I leave to my wife, who is younger and more technically inclined. Come to think of it, I sometimes wonder if she isn't more fond of her PC than she is of me (maybe that's another reason I don't like computers!) Nevertheless, it is undeniable that more and more people have PCs, and presumably most know how to get the best out of them. So – even though I can't claim much first-hand experience or expertise – I have dutifully done my research, and spent a day surfing birding websites. I also have spoken with many birders about their computer experiences.

## To surf or not to surf

I don't actually recommend random searching and surfing. Try typing in "birds" or "birdwatching" and you'll soon see what I mean. You'll be faced with a list of literally hundreds of sites and to visit them all would take weeks. Moreover, you'll soon realize that quite a high percentage refer to cage birds and pets, and a fair number are nothing to do with birds at all (everything from golf to soft porn!). A far more productive process is to visit a specific site that you already know and then use the chain method – other recommended related sites – to lead you further. You will find that just about all the organizations featured in the birdwatching magazines have websites, so it's easy to get started. There is also a list of some of them on page 136 of this book. However, this technology is moving at such a pace that it really would be pointless to give lots of detailed information, as much of it would become out-of-date almost immediately.

There are masses of bird-related websites that you can now visit, which will not only offer information (in many cases frequently updated) but will also allow you to download text, videos, and illustrations. However – a warning from my computerized chums – remember that if you do intend to download, then you need a computer powerful enough to handle the process. Otherwise you may be in for some long frustrating sessions, clicking away on your mouse and muttering at your screen, until you finally realize you need to buy more memory, not to mention a scanner and a new colour printer, etc.

## Keeping records

A lot of birders use their PC to keep a record of their sightings. I keep my Hampstead Heath records on my word processor so that I can more easily edit and print out a sort of report at the end of the year. On the other hand, I also keep my big notebook, in which I add drawings and photos and a rather fuller account of my days out. Call me old fashioned, but I find this more personal than the computerized version, but there is certainly a place for both methods.

Another major advantage of a computer is, of course, easy correspondence. Email is a

*Right: Barn owl – can look like something from outer space! I don't find sitting and surfing on the net as thrilling as seeing a spectacular bird like this out in the open.*

fantastic way of exchanging views and information and simply making contact. Unfortunately, I believe that there is some evidence that it is perhaps a little too easy! We often hear of email exchanges that proliferate and escalate to the level of a bombardment. I'm sure you have read of such things in the papers (or maybe you've had personal experience yourself). Well, the bird world is certainly not immune! Already on the competitive twitching scene there have been controversies and arguments that have involved accusations, threats of litigation, hoax and poison pen emails (or should that be poison keyboard?) Obviously, you won't be getting involved with that kind of thing! Or maybe you will, if only to marvel (or despair) at what an extremist image birdwatchers sometimes project.

What I want to say is that there is some excellent information out there in birdwatching cyberspace, but there is also some pretty strange and abstruse stuff. Don't let it put you off. The point of the hobby is to get out in the fresh air, not to sit staring at a computer screen for hours on end. The new technology is unarguably incredible: by all means use it. Go virtual birding if you like, but – be honest – it will never beat the real thing.

## And finally

Birdwatching can be whatever you want it to be: feeding birds in the garden, twitching, local patch watching, a holiday pursuit, an obsession or an occasional distraction. It really doesn't matter. Don't judge yourself, or worry about being judged by others. Enjoy, on whatever level feels right for you. Oh, and whilst you're at it, don't ignore the rest of the natural world: insects, animals, wildflowers etc. Oh yes, and people. We're all in it together!

# WEBSITES

Here are just a few of the many birding websites; only by visiting them will you discover which ones really interest you. Certainly, if you become enticed by twitching and want rare bird news, you will want to visit the relevant sites and phone local or national birdlines. The services they provide are excellent, with news of rare birds updated several times a day.

## National conservation organizations

The Royal Society for the Protection of Birds (RSPB) – **www.rspb.org.uk**

RSPB – The Wildlife Explorers – **www.rspb.org.uk/youth/**

The Wildlife Trusts – **www.wildlifetrusts.org**

Wildlife Watch – **www.wildlifetrusts.org**

The Wildfowl & Wetlands Trust – **www.wwt.org.uk**

British Trust for Ornithology (BTO) – **www.bto.org/index.htm**

## Birding and nature magazines

British Birds – **www.britishbirds.co.uk**

Birdwatch – **www.birdwatch.co.uk**

Birding World – **www.birdingworld.freeserve.co.uk/**

BBC Natural History – **www.bbc.co.uk/nature**

## Online birding magazines

Birds of Britain – **www.birdsofbritain.co.uk**

## The British Birdwatching Fair

**www.birdfair.org.uk**

## Disabled Birders

Disabled Birders Association (UK) – **www.disabledbirdersassociation.org.uk**

## Online shopping: birding books, bird food, etc.

**www.amazon.co.uk**

**www.bol.co.uk**

**www.jjstroud.freeserve.co.uk**

**www.birdguides.com**

**www.birdcare.com/birdon/**

## Other bird and birding-related websites

Fatbirder – **www.fatbirder.com**

Conservation and birdwatching in Scotland – **www.wildlifeweb.f9.co.uk**

Raptor Conservation– **www.raptor.uk.com**

Euro BirdNet United Kingdom – **www.osme.org/ebn/index.html**

BirdWeb – **www.birdweb.co.uk**

Birdlinks United Kingdom – **www.skof.se/lank/europa/storbritannien.htm**

The British Library National Sound Archive – **www.bl.uk/collections/sound-archive/wild**

## Magazines

British Birds – **www.britishbirds.co.uk**

Birdwatch – **www.birdwatch.co.uk**

Birding World – **www.birdingworld.freeserve.co.uk**

# MAGAZINES

There has never been an easier time to get information on birdwatching (well, to get information on anything actually I suppose). It is strange for me to think back to the time when I first started birding as an early teenager, when the only identification book available was the Observer's Book of Birds! It was a nice little book (still in print I believe) but it only had about forty species in it. Similarly, for many years the only bird magazine available was British Birds (happily, still going strong), which – let's face it – was and still is definitely for "real birdwatchers". Nowadays, you have a choice of several excellent magazines suitable for varying levels of expertise, all with high quality artwork, news and articles, and masses of adverts for optical equipment, outdoor clothing, books, videos, holidays, etc. I do very strongly recommend that you subscribe to at least one of these magazines and do contact or visit the specialist dealers for whatever you happen to be after. These companies are almost invariably run by birdwatchers for birdwatchers, and you will benefit from honest expert advice, and probably cheaper prices than the high street shops.

## British Birds

The Banks
Mountfield
Nr Robertsbridge
East Sussex
TN32 5JY
Tel: 01580 882039

## Birdwatch

Solo Publishing Ltd
3D/F Leroy House
436 Essex Road, Islington
London
N1 3QP
Tel: 0207 704 9495

## Birdwatching

Bretton Court
Peterborough
PE3 8DZ
Tel: 01733 264 666

## Birding World

Stonerunner
Coast Road
Cley next the Sea
Holt
Norfolk
NR25 7RY

# ORGANIZATIONS

## Royal Society for the Protection of Birds (RSPB)

**UK Headquarters**

The Lodge

Sandy

Bedfordshire

SG19 2DL

Tel: 01767 680551

Email: **bird@rspb.demon.co.uk**


**Scotland Headquarters**

Dunedin House

25 Ravelston Terrace

Edinburgh

EH4 3TP

Tel: 0131 311 6500


**Northern Ireland Headquarters**

Belvoir Park Forest

Belfast

BT8 4QT

Tel: 01232 491547


**South Wales**

Sutherland House

Castlebridge

Cowbridge Road East

Cardiff

CF11 9AB

Tel: 02920 353000

## Wildfowl & Wetlands Trust

WWT Slimbridge

Gloucestershire

GL2 7BT

Tel: 01453 891900

Email: **enquiries@wwt.org.uk**

## British Trust for Ornithology (BTO)

The National Centre for Ornithology

The Nunnery

Thetford

Norfolk

IP24 2PU

Tel: 01842 750 050

Email: **general@bto.org**

## The Wildlife Trusts

The Kiln

Waterside

Mather Road

Newark

Nottinghamshire

NG24 1WT

Tel: 01636 677711

Email: **info@wildlife-trusts.cix.co.uk**

# FURTHER READING

*Bill Oddie's Birds of Britain and Ireland*, Bill Oddie
(New Holland, 1998)

*Bill Oddie's Birding Pack*, Bill Oddie
(New Holland, 2001)

*Bill Oddie's Birding Map of Britain and Ireland*, Bill Oddie
(New Holland, 2001)

*The Complete Garden Bird Book*, Mark Golley with Stephen Moss
(New Holland, 1996)

*Collins Field Guide to the Birds of Britain and Europe*,
K. Mullarney, L. Svensson, D. Zetterstrom, P. Grant
(Harper Collins, 1999)

*Top Birding Spots in Britain and Ireland*, David Tipling
(Harper Collins, 1996)

# GLOSSARY

**Axillaries**: Underwing feathers at the base of the wing forming the so-called 'armpits'.

**Coverts**: Feathers on the upper and lower surfaces of the wing that assist streamlining in flight.

**Eye-stripe**: Tract of feathers that runs through the eye.

**Flight feathers**: Feathers used for flight; the outer primaries and the inner secondaries of the wings.

**Irruption**: Mass movement of a population from one area to another, usually in response to the exhaustion of food supply. Waxwings are a good example.

**Juvenile**: A young bird in its full plumage.

**Lek**: Communal display area used by males of certain species such as Black Grouse and Ruff.

**Mantle**: The feathers on the back.

**Migration**: The movement by some species from one area to another, such as the Swallow from its wintering grounds in southern Africa to its breeding grounds in Europe.

**Moult**: Because feathers become worn and damaged, they are shed regularly and replaced by new ones.

**Passage migrant**: A migrant bird that is seen when it stops off to rest and feed while migrating from its breeding grounds to its wintering quarters.

**Passerine**: A large and extensive group of birds with the ability to perch.

**Pelagics**: Oceanic seawatching trips usually involving boat.

**Plumes**: Long, showy feathers often acquired at the start of the breeding season and used for display, such as those shown by egrets.

**Race**: Distinctive populations of the same species which are usually isolated geographically and show visible, albeit often subtle, plumage differences.

**Raptor**: Diurnal birds of prey.

**Resident**: Present within an area throughout the year, such as the Robin.

**Species**: Genetically distinct individuals, which can breed together and produce viable offspring. However, many species can interbreed and produce viable hybrids, especially ducks.

**Speculum**: Shiny area of feathering on the secondary flight feathers of many ducks.

**Summer plumage**: The plumage acquired at the start of the breeding season.

**Supercilium**: The tract of feathers that runs above the eye and eye-stripe as a distinct stripe, such as that shown by the Sedge Warbler.

**Tube-noses**: A group of seabirds, with distinctive nostrils, including petrels, shearwaters and fulmars, the last being capable of discharging a pungent, oily substance.

**Wader**: A group of birds with long legs and bills, often found around the shoreline, including sandpipers, plovers and curlews.

**Wildfowl**: The family of birds comprising swans, geese and ducks.

**Wingspan**: The distance between wingtips when fully stretched in flight.

**Winter plumage**: The plumage seen during the non-breeding winter months.

# INDEX

Page numbers in **bold** refer to illustrations

# ACKNOWLEDGEMENTS

All photographs by David M. Cottridge, with the exception of the following:

Rene H. de Heer (Windrush Photos) p49(l)

Mike Wilkes p59(t,b)

Chris Gomersall p78

Roger Wilmshurst pp88, 91

Tom Ennis p120

David Kjaer pp126, 131

Chris Packham p130

(t= top; b=bottom; c=centre; l=left; r=right)